SPORTS MEDICINE

SCIENCE • TECHNOLOGY • ENGINEERING

BY JOSH GREGORY

CHILDREN'S PRESS®

An Imprint of Scholastic Inc.

CONTENT CONSULTANT
Brian Parr, PhD, Associate Professor, Department of Exercise and Sports Medicine,
University of South Carolina Aiken

PHOTOGRAPHS ©: cover: Stanislaw Pytel/Getty Images; 3: Kzenon/Shutterstock, Inc.; 4 left: H.M. Herget/
National Geographic Creative; 4 right: Tribune Content Agency LLC/Alamy Images; 5 left: Rocketclips, Inc./
Shutterstock, Inc.; 5 right: Image Point Fr/Shutterstock, Inc.; 6: Xinhua/Alamy Images; 8: Stock Connection/
Superstock, Inc.; 9: Ojo Images/Superstock, Inc.; 10: Interfoto/Alamy Images; 11 top: H.M. Herget/
National Geographic Creative; 11 bottom: Imagno/The Image Works; 12: Mary Evans Picture Library/
The Image Works; 13: Everett Collection/Superstock, Inc.; 14 top: Peter Read Miller/Sports Illustrated/
Getty Images; 14 bottom: B. Leighty/Alamy Images; 15: Brand Affinity Technologies, Inc. via Getty Images;
16: Westend61/Superstock, Inc.; 17: Ivan Nesterov/Alamy Images; 18: Paul Bradbury/Media Bakery;
20: motorolka/Shutterstock, Inc.; 21: Tom/Dee Ann McCarthy/Media Bakery; 22 left: Everett Collection
Historical/Alamy Images; 22 right-23 bottom: Cultura Limited/Superstock, Inc.; 23 top: Radius Images/
Alamy Images; 24: ERproductions Ltd/Media Bakery; 25: Zuma Press, Inc/Alamy Images; 26: Tribune
Content Agency LLC/Alamy Images; 27: Loren Elliott/Missourian via AP Images; 28 left: Peter Macdiarmid/
Getty Images; 28 right: Chase Jarvis/Getty Images; 29 left: Avpics/Alamy Images; 29 right: Yves Logghe/
AP Images; 30: Javier Larrea/Media Bakery; 31: Westend61/Superstock, Inc.; 32: Jim Craigmyle/Media
Bakery; 34: Rocketclips, Inc./Shutterstock, Inc.; 35: Amelie-Benoist/Superstock, Inc.; 36: kali9/Getty
Images; 37: Agencja Fotograficzna Caro/Alamy Images; 38 left: Maridav/Shutterstock, Inc.; 38 right: Marco
Govel/Shutterstock, Inc.; 39: Ramon Espelt Photography/Shutterstock, Inc.; 40: Solis Images/Shutterstock,
Inc.; 41: Phanie/Superstock, Inc.; 42: Courtesy of Darin Swan; 44: Hero Images/Media Bakery; 45:
wavebreakmedia/Shutterstock, Inc.; 46: Blulz60/Shutterstock, Inc.; 48: Image Point Fr/Shutterstock, Inc.;
49: Patryk Kosmider/Shutterstock, Inc.; 50 top: Nucleus Medical Art Inc/Alamy Images; 50 bottom-51
bottom: piotrwzk/Shutterstock, Inc.; 51 top: Ted Horowitz/Media Bakery; 52: Monika Wisniewska/
Shutterstock, Inc.; 53: Robert Kneschke/Shutterstock, Inc.; 54 left: Alex Trautwig/Getty Images; 54 right:
wavebreakmedia/Shutterstock, Inc.; 55: Bettina Strenske/Alamy Images; 56: Kelly Redinger/Media Bakery;
57: Florian Kopp/Superstock, Inc.; 58: Kzenon/Shutterstock, Inc.; 59: Tribune Content Agency LLC/Alamy
Images.

LIBRARY OF CONGRESS CATALOGING-IN-PUBLICATION DATA
Gregory, Josh, author.
 Sports medicine : science, technology, engineering / by Josh Gregory.
    pages cm. — (Calling all innovators: a career for you)
 ISBN 978-0-531-23004-6 (library binding) — ISBN 978-0-531-23222-4 (pbk.)
1. Sports medicine—Juvenile literature. 2. Sports medicine—Vocational guidance—Juvenile literature.
3. Sports physicians—Juvenile literature. I. Title. II. Series: Calling all innovators.
 RC1210.G74 2016
 617.1'027023—dc23   2015029115

All rights reserved. Published in 2016 by Children's Press, an imprint of Scholastic Inc.
Printed in the United States of America 113

1 2 3 4 5 6 7 8 9 10 R 25 24 23 22 21 20 19 18 17 16

Science, technology, engineering, the arts, and math are the fields that drive innovation. Whether they are finding ways to make our lives easier or developing the latest entertainment, the people who work in these fields are changing the world for the better. Do you have what it takes to join the ranks of today's greatest innovators? Read on to discover if a career in the exciting world of sports medicine is for you.

TABLE *of* CONTENTS

The ancient Greek doctor Hippocrates made great advancements in medicine.

CHAPTER ONE

A Special Kind of Medicine **7**

CHAPTER TWO

Treating Today's Athletes **19**

A robotic exoskeleton can help people learn to walk again after major injuries.

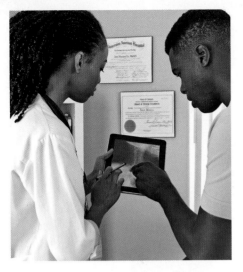

A doctor uses an x-ray to explain an injury to her patient.

CHAPTER THREE

It Takes a
Team 33

AN INTERVIEW WITH

Physical Therapist
Darin Swan 42

CHAPTER FOUR

Getting Back
in the
Game 47

A doctor examines a patient to diagnose a knee injury.

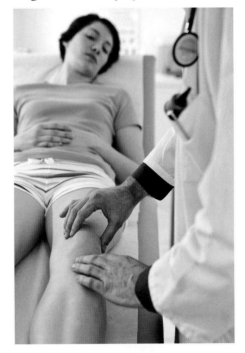

CAREER STATS 60
RESOURCES 61
GLOSSARY 62
INDEX 63
ABOUT THE AUTHOR 64

Basketball star Derrick Rose has suffered several injuries to his knees and ankles over the course of his career.

KNEE BRACE HELPS PROTECT AGAINST FUTURE INJURY

1

A SPECIAL KIND OF MEDICINE

During a professional football game, a quarterback suffers a **concussion** when a defending player tackles him violently to the ground. After her morning jog, a woman who has run regularly for years notices a new pain in her legs. While playing basketball in the park with friends, a teenage boy twists his ankle as he comes down from grabbing a rebound. A young girl loses control of her skateboard while jumping off a ramp and breaks her arm by trying to prevent her fall.

These are just a few of the many injuries that can affect people who exercise or play sports. Some sports injuries are sudden, while others set in over time. Some can have serious, lasting effects, while others are easy to treat. Thankfully, there is an entire branch of medicine devoted to dealing with the injuries athletes face.

CREATING A NEW FIELD

ca. 444 BCE	1928	1954	1989
Iccus of Tarentum writes the first book about athletic training methods.	The term sports medicine is coined.	The American College of Sports Medicine is founded.	The American Board of Medical Specialties officially recognizes sports medicine as a specialty.

AT PLAY AND AT RISK

Throughout history, athletic activity has been a major part of life for people all around the world. It provides the exercise people need to maintain healthy bodies. Many athletes enjoy the thrill of competition or the exhilarating rush of pulling off a difficult task. They take pleasure in setting goals and improving their abilities. Sports can also play an important role in a person's social life. Some athletes are even able to turn their abilities into full-time careers. Though there are many advantages to participating in sports, every kind of athletic activity presents some risk of injury. Even people who are in very good physical shape can be hurt while playing sports or exercising.

Sports and exercise have existed for thousands of years. But there has not always been a specialized branch of medicine devoted to the injuries they produce. Instead, people had to rely on doctors who did not always fully understand the special needs of an athlete.

An ancient illustration portrays women playing a game similar to golf.

Runners move their bodies in ways that most people don't need to in their daily lives.

DIFFERENT DAMAGE

Sports injuries are often very different from other medical issues. People in many sports and exercise activities move and put stress on their bodies in ways that would not happen in normal situations. For example, the average person does not go through the throwing motions that a baseball pitcher performs dozens of times every day. And unlike professional football players, most people are not usually tackled to the ground on a regular basis.

Additionally, when athletes are injured, they do not simply want to heal enough to return to everyday life. They want to go back to their physical activities as soon as they can. They also want to be just as effective as they were before being hurt. A treatment that leaves the patient with a weaker body or makes him or her vulnerable to further injury might be fine for some people. For an athlete, however, it could be devastating.

FIRST THINGS FIRST

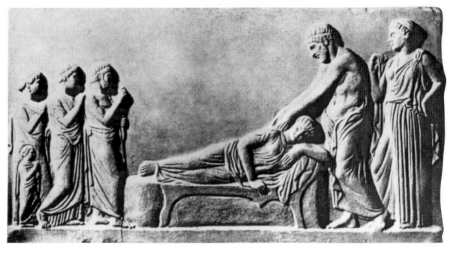

Ancient carvings and other artifacts illustrate the methods and treatments used in medicine long ago.

HEALTH CARE THROUGHOUT HISTORY

Today, medicine is a highly refined science. Doctors have a strong understanding of how the human body works and have developed effective treatments for countless illnesses and injuries. However, this has not always been the case. Modern medical professionals, whether they focus on sports or not, rely on a body of knowledge that scientists and doctors have built over the course of thousands of years.

EARLY TREATMENTS

Prehistoric people did not have a scientific understanding of the body. They often believed that illnesses came from such sources as demons or gods. People sometimes attempted to cure medical conditions by praying or performing rituals. Other times, they used treatments of homemade plant-based medications.

Over time, people gained more knowledge. Just as doctors do today, ancient **physicians** cut open dead bodies to examine their inner workings. The researchers began to piece together information on how different organs and systems related to different functions. In ancient civilizations across Asia, Egypt, Greece, and the Middle East, doctors developed a variety of surgical techniques and medications. They wrote about their findings and passed their knowledge down from generation to generation.

Hippocrates consults with a patient in ancient Greece.

THE NEXT STEPS

One of the most famous doctors of the ancient world was the Greek physician Hippocrates. Born sometime around 460 BCE, Hippocrates vocally disagreed with the belief that gods and demons caused illnesses. He realized that factors such as a patient's diet and living conditions played an important role in health. Hippocrates was also the author of a code of medical ethics that doctors still follow today.

Further medical developments came with changes in technology that made it easier to study and treat the body. For example, the microscope was invented in the late 16th century. This tool allowed scientists to observe bacteria, viruses, and other tiny life-forms that can cause illnesses. Armed with better knowledge of how sicknesses spread, doctors began finding more effective treatments and cures. They also discovered ways to prevent many illnesses from spreading in the first place.

GETTING BETTER ALL THE TIME

The medical field is constantly evolving. Medicine is more effective today than it has ever been. However, there is still a lot to learn about the human body and the many conditions that can affect it. Medical experts around the world conduct studies, experiment with new treatments, and develop new medications and technology. These innovators push science forward and make the world a better place. Illnesses that are deadly today could one day be easily treatable. As with all scientific progress, it can be difficult to predict the future. Almost anything is possible! ✳

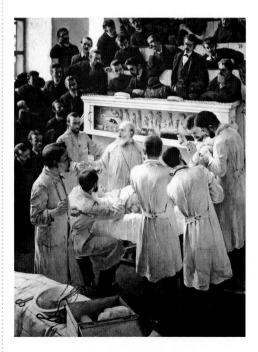

Our understanding of medicine improved significantly in the 19th and 20th centuries.

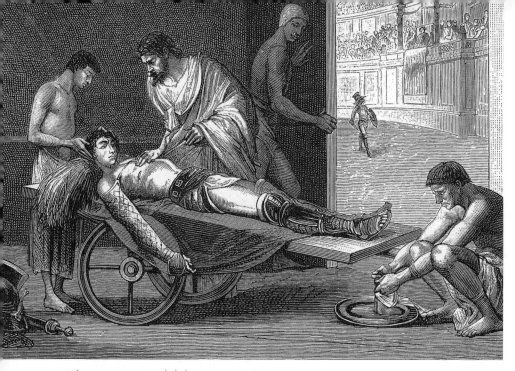

A doctor treats an injured gladiator in ancient Rome.

ANCIENT ATHLETES

Sports have probably existed since the dawn of human civilization. **Archaeologists** have uncovered evidence that people played ball games thousands of years ago in China and in the Aztec Empire of Central America. Ancient people also participated in footraces and contests of hunting or battle skills, such as wrestling and archery. In 776 BCE, the ancient Greeks introduced the Olympic Games. These are often seen as the earliest form of modern, organized sports. Held every four years, the Olympics allowed Greece's greatest athletes to compete in a variety of athletic contests.

In ancient Rome, gladiator battles were extremely popular spectator sports. Thousands of fans packed arenas to watch skilled warriors battle each other or fight against wild animals. These contests were very dangerous, and gladiators were regularly injured. By the second century CE, some doctors had begun specializing in treatments for these warrior-athletes.

A NEW FIELD

Over the following centuries, more people began participating in athletic activities. At the same time, doctors and scientists learned more about the benefits of exercise and the limits of the human body. In addition, a new version of the Olympic Games was begun in the late 1800s. These games allowed athletes across the globe to compete against one another every four years. By the early 20th century, sports were a bigger part of life than ever before. There were professional leagues around the world for a wide variety of sports.

Nevertheless, sports medicine was still not formally recognized as its own field of medicine. In fact, it was not until 1928 that the term *sports medicine* was used for the first time. That year, doctors from around the world gathered in Switzerland to form the world's first sports medicine organization. In the following decades, more medical professionals started to specialize in treating athletes. Sports teams began employing their own medical teams, and doctors began opening up specialized sports medicine clinics.

Runners compete in a hurdles event at the 1932 Olympic Games in Los Angeles, California.

CLAUDIUS GALEN

Claudius Galen (ca. 130 to ca. 210 CE) is thought to be one of the first doctors to focus his efforts on helping athletes. In his home city of Pergamum, Greece, he worked closely with local gladiators. Over time, he became renowned for his ability to treat their wounds. This led him to move to Rome's capital city, where he served as the personal physician to three consecutive Roman emperors. Galen's theories and methods continued to influence the practice of medicine for hundreds of years.

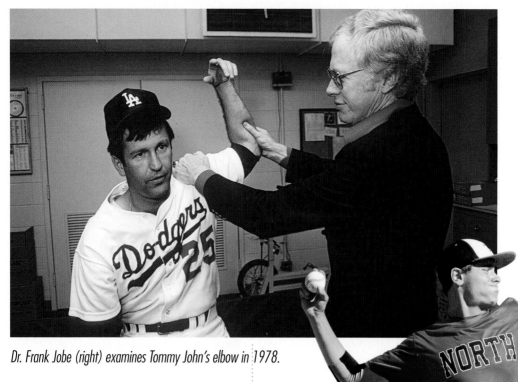

Dr. Frank Jobe (right) examines Tommy John's elbow in 1978.

PLAY BALL!

Over the course of a baseball game, a pitcher might throw the ball up to 100 times. Each one of these throws puts tremendous stress on the pitcher's elbow. Over time, this stress sometimes leads to a sudden tear in the pitcher's ulnar collateral **ligament** (UCL). A torn UCL can dramatically affect the pitcher's performance on the mound. It was once considered a career-ending injury. That all changed, however, in the 1970s.

TOMMY JOHN

In 1974, Tommy John was a star pitcher for the Los Angeles Dodgers. But that year, in the middle of a promising season, he tore his UCL. John thought his major league career was over. However, the situation turned out better than he could have ever hoped.

Dr. Frank Jobe was a well-respected **orthopedic** surgeon who had worked with the Dodgers for many years. On September 25, 1974, Dr. Jobe performed a new surgical technique on John's injured elbow. He first removed a **tendon** from John's right arm. Then he used this healthy tendon to replace the ruined ligament in John's left arm. John sat out the following season. He spent the time

strengthening his arm and learning a new way to pitch that put less stress on his elbow. Amazingly, John returned to the mound in 1976. He continued playing pro baseball until he retired in 1989. Even more astounding was that John pitched better after his recovery than he had in the seasons before he was injured.

AN ORDINARY PROCEDURE

Tommy John's extraordinary recovery proved that Dr. Jobe's new technique was a major breakthrough. Since then, the procedure has been called Tommy John surgery. Countless baseball players of all levels have benefited from it. Jobe himself performed the procedure more than 1,000 times throughout the rest of his career. Today, Tommy John surgery is a common part of baseball, and it has a high success rate.

Pitchers bend their elbows in a way that can easily cause injury.

Tommy John's full recovery allowed him to have a long career as a major league pitcher.

Knee injuries are common for many athletes.

COMMON SPORTS INJURIES

Over the following decades, sports medicine became widely recognized as a distinct field of medicine. Doctors, trainers, therapists, and other experts have developed sophisticated ways to deal with the countless injuries athletes suffer. Amazingly, issues that would once have ended a career or decreased a player's performance are now treatable with routine procedures.

Most sports injuries involve muscles, joints, or bones. Athletic activity puts a lot of stress on these parts of the body. In many sports, one wrong move can cause an athlete to overextend himself or herself, resulting in a tear or break. One common injury in soccer, basketball, and many other sports is a tear in the anterior cruciate ligament (ACL). The ACL is a connective piece of the knee joint. When an athlete stretches it too far, it can suddenly tear. This injury may leave an athlete unable to stand without assistance. However, it can be treated rather easily through surgery and therapy.

Other sports injuries develop over long periods of time. For example, golfers and tennis players can develop tendinosis in their elbows. Tendinosis is the result of many very small injuries to a tendon. Performing the same motion too often without giving the tendon enough rest to heal is one cause. It can also be a result of using poor form. The condition causes pain and stiffness in a joint. It can be treated over time through physical therapy.

Not all sports injuries involve muscles, bones, or joints. Boxers, football players, and other athletes are at risk of brain injuries. One of the most common is a concussion. This minor brain injury comes as a result of a jolt to the head. It can leave a person temporarily dizzy, confused, or nauseous. It may also affect physical coordination. Sports doctors keep a close eye on people who suffer concussions to make sure the condition doesn't become more serious. If someone experiences a second concussion before the first has fully healed, he or she may lose consciousness or even die from the injuries.

Though boxers wear padded gloves, head injuries are still extremely common in the sport.

Bicycling may have risks, but sports medicine professionals know that good exercise habits and safety precautions can prevent injury.

PROTECTIVE HELMETS HELP PREVENT HEAD INJURIES

2

TREATING TODAY'S ATHLETES

Today, sports medicine is a bigger field than it's ever been. Most people participate in athletic activities at some point in their lives. It may be a low-intensity exercise to stay in shape or the intense workout of a high-level athlete. While physical activity has its risks, it is an important part of a healthy lifestyle. For this reason, sports medicine professionals do not just treat injuries. They also develop ways people can avoid injury while still incorporating athletic activities into their lives. Many work with athletes to help them improve their performance, too.

As the field of sports medicine has grown, the methods used to treat injuries have improved. Today's medical professionals take advantage of the latest technology to help patients recover. They also refine their techniques continually to provide the best care possible.

TECHNOLOGICAL BREAKTHROUGHS

1895	1987	1992	2010
X-rays are discovered.	Platelet-rich plasma is used for the first time.	The antigravity treadmill is patented.	The eLEGS™ robotic exoskeleton is introduced.

IT'S ELECTRIC!

Many common sports injuries develop from body parts rubbing against each other. Over time, this can cause **inflammation**. For example, joints such as the shoulder, hip, elbow, and knee have small sacs of fluid called bursae. They provide padding as a joint's bones, muscles, and tendons flex and extend. However, repetitive motions like the ones athletes perform can cause the bursae to become inflamed, a condition known as bursitis. This can be very painful.

Inflammation is easily treated with medicine, but reaching bursae or other internal body parts usually requires an injection. This can hurt and might leave a bruise. However, sports doctors recently developed a new method of delivering medicine to inflamed areas. It is called iontophoresis. Doctors first put special liquid medication onto a patient's skin. Then they place an electrode on top of the medication. Its electrical charge pushes the medicine down into the skin. The process is painless, and it does not leave a bruise or any other damage to surrounding tissue. Another technique called phonophoresis works much the same way. It uses sound waves instead of electricity.

Iontophoresis can help reduce pain in patients with inflammation.

ELECTRODES

To create platelet-rich plasma, doctors must first take a blood sample from a patient.

PLATELET-RICH PLASMA

For a high-level or professional athlete, a lengthy recovery can slow down or even end a promising career. In team sports, an injured player can also affect the entire team. If a star player is forced to stay on the sidelines during a big game, his or her team may struggle to compete effectively.

As a result, sports medicine experts are always searching for new ways to speed up the healing process. One of the latest techniques in this area involves a substance called platelet-rich plasma. Platelet-rich plasma is found naturally in human blood. By taking a blood sample from a patient and spinning it rapidly in a special machine, doctors can separate the plasma from the rest of the blood. The plasma is then injected into the part of a patient's body that needs to heal. These injections are believed to lower pain and speed up the body's natural healing process.

Though scientists are not quite sure why the treatment works or how effective it really is, many sports doctors swear by it. Professional athletes such as golfer Tiger Woods, National Football League (NFL) player Troy Polamalu, and tennis superstar Rafael Nadal have all used platelet-rich plasma to help injuries heal.

FROM THIS TO THAT

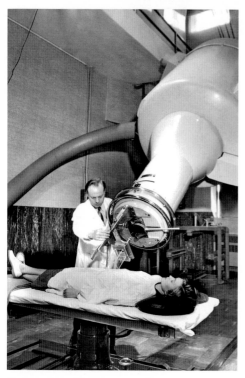

Early x-ray machines were very large.

TAKING A LOOK INSIDE

The first step in treating any medical condition is to correctly **diagnose** the issue. Part of this involves simply listening to a patient's complaints and performing some basic tests. Sometimes doctors also need an up close look to figure out the necessary details of a situation. But how can they investigate injuries that lie deep within a patient's body? Thanks to modern medical imaging technology, it is a lot easier than you might imagine.

X-RAY

Today, there are many forms of medical imaging available to doctors. Each method has its own benefits and drawbacks. The earliest example is the x-ray. Discovered in 1895 by the German physicist Wilhelm Conrad Röntgen, x-rays are a type of **radiation**. When aimed at the human body, they pass through soft tissue such as skin and muscle. But they do not pass through hard material such as bones. Photographic film is placed behind a person as x-rays pass through them. The film captures an image of the skeleton. This

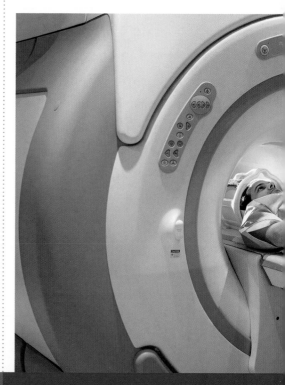

allows doctors to closely examine broken bones and other injuries. Despite its age, x-ray technology is still used today.

ULTRASOUND

One of the most commonly used forms of medical imaging today is ultrasound. Instead of radiation, ultrasound uses sound waves to create an image of the body's interior. High doses of radiation can cause medical problems. For this reason, ultrasound imaging carries fewer risks for a patient than x-rays do.

In ultrasound, a medical professional touches a patient's skin with a device called a transducer. The transducer projects sound

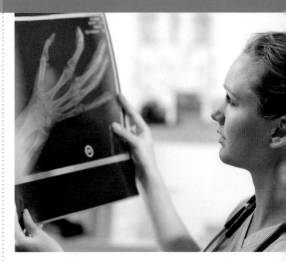

Radiologists are doctors who specialize in reading medical images.

waves into the patient's body, and they bounce back to the transducer. This creates an image on an attached monitor. The transducer can be easily moved around to provide a range of viewing angles. It can even provide a moving image of the body's interior in action. This is helpful for observing blood flow and other processes.

MAGNETIC RESONANCE IMAGING

Magnetic resonance imaging (MRI) is another popular way to take a look inside the body. It uses magnetic fields and radio waves to create an image. An MRI's main advantage is that it can show certain types of tissue that do not show up on other kinds of scans. For example, it picks up ligaments and tendons, which are especially important in the field of sports medicine. ✳

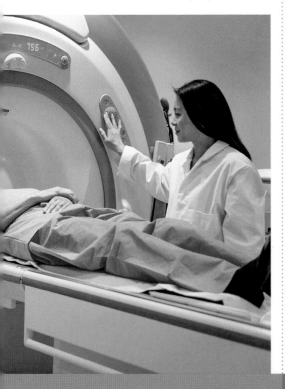

MRI technology is often used to examine a patient's brain.

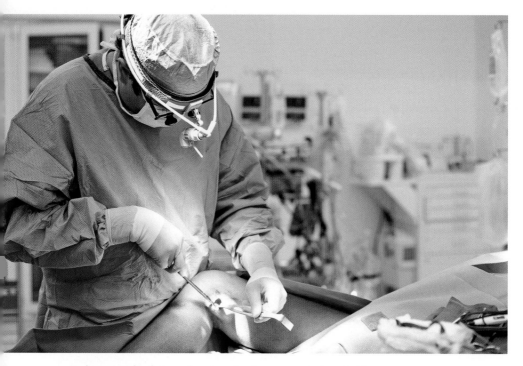

Modern surgical techniques do not require doctors to make large incisions to treat common traumas such as knee injuries.

SUPERB SURGERY

Sports doctors usually try to avoid performing surgery unless it is absolutely necessary. Surgical procedures can be painful, and they sometimes expose a patient to further risks. They can also require a long recovery time. However, many injuries leave doctors with no choice but to operate. Thankfully, modern techniques make most sports-related surgeries much less unpleasant for patients than they were in the past. For example, new methods allow surgeons to make fewer and smaller cuts in a patient's body during procedures. This means the patient will experience less pain. It also shortens recovery times, enabling athletes to be back in action sooner. In addition, modern medications and **sterilization** techniques have greatly reduced the risk of infections from surgery.

FLOATING IN SPACE

As they recover from injuries, athletes undergo physical therapy. This helps them regain strength and mobility and get back into competitive shape. Like training for a sport, physical therapy involves exercise and hard work. Even the simplest exercises can be difficult for someone recovering from a major injury. For example, an athlete who receives ankle surgery might have difficulty walking or jogging on a treadmill during therapy. The weight of his or her body might be too much for the healing joint to handle.

Antigravity treadmills can help patients with these kinds of conditions. Originally developed for use by astronauts, the antigravity treadmill uses an inflatable air chamber to support the weight of patients' bodies as they run, making them feel lighter. It can be adjusted to put more weight back on patients' legs over time. This allows people recovering from lower body injuries to gradually build up strength.

INFLATABLE AIR CHAMBER
SUPPORTS PATIENT'S
WEIGHT

Antigravity treadmills help recovering athletes get back on the move soon after an injury.

LEARNING TO MOVE AGAIN

Neurological damage is a serious issue for many athletes. A blow to the head or spine can cause a wide range of problems. A brain injury could leave an athlete mentally impaired. Neurological damage can also affect a person's ability to control his or her body. In some cases, the patient must relearn how to walk. This is an incredibly difficult thing to do. However, new technology is making it a little easier.

Today, patients with leg **paralysis** can wear a robotic suit that helps them stand and walk. The suit moves the body and forces each leg to take a step forward as patients shift their weight. This helps patients remember what it feels like to walk. Over time, the therapist can adjust the device to give patients more control over their steps. Gradually, patients learn to stand and walk without assistance.

BATTERY-POWERED EXOSKELETON

Though robotic exoskeletons may seem like science fiction, they are helping people learn to walk again.

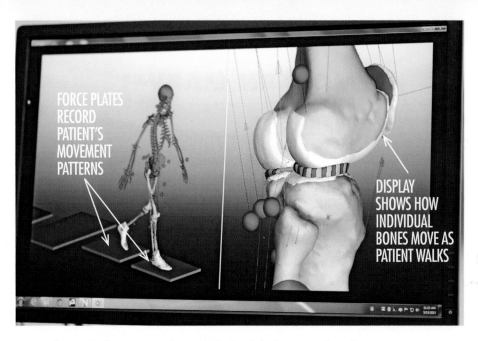

FORCE PLATES RECORD PATIENT'S MOVEMENT PATTERNS

DISPLAY SHOWS HOW INDIVIDUAL BONES MOVE AS PATIENT WALKS

Gait analysis technology can provide extremely detailed information about the way a patient moves.

WATCHING PATIENTS WALK

Doctors, trainers, and therapists can learn a lot about patients by observing the way they move. This is known as **gait** analysis. For example, a runner's feet might hit the ground in a way that hurts his or her ankles. Or a person might run with an inward bend in his or her leg that could damage the knee. Poor posture can cause back pain. Medical professionals can correct such issues by teaching the patient to maintain a proper form while moving.

Technology can help bring out hard-to-see details in a gait analysis. Sometimes therapists make video recordings of patients' movements and play them back in slow motion. They might also use force plates. As a patient walks on these plates, the devices record information about the person's footsteps and movement patterns. This information is sent to a computer so the therapist can analyze it. Gait analysis can also be performed using computerized motion-capture technology. This is very similar to the motion capture used to create computer animation and video games.

MODERN MARVEL

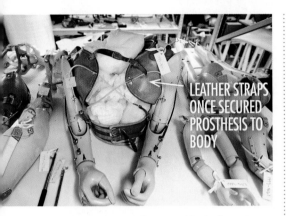

LEATHER STRAPS ONCE SECURED PROSTHESIS TO BODY

Early prostheses were heavy and had a limited range of motion.

THE LATEST LIMBS

The loss of a limb is a devastating event. It can be especially traumatic for athletes, who often rely on every part of the body to compete effectively. Someone who loses part of an arm or leg is often fitted with a device called a **prosthesis**. The prosthesis acts as a replacement. In the past, prostheses were often made of materials such as wood, metal, and leather. These devices were heavy and uncomfortable. Thanks to the work of engineers and scientists, modern limb replacements have advanced considerably. They are now lightweight and highly mobile. Some have built-in systems to absorb the shock, or force, of walking, running, and jumping. Others are even equipped with computer technology that automatically adjusts to different types of terrain.

AMPUTEE ATHLETES

Amputees have competed as runners and cyclists, and in countless other sports. The best of these athletes compete in the Paralympic Games. Like the Olympics, the Paralympics is an international competition among some of the world's greatest athletes and its games are held every four years.

Many athletes who have lost limbs participate in the same legendary activities that challenge able-bodied athletes. Such accomplishments have included scaling the 29,035-foot (8,850-meter) Mount Everest. In 2010, Philippe Croizon swam across

Activities such as skiing are no longer off-limits to amputees.

CURVED SHAPE
HELPS RUNNERS
MAKE NATURAL
MOVEMENTS

A double-amputee runner participates in the 2014 London Marathon.

the English Channel in only 13.5 hours. The more than 20-mile (32-kilometer) trip is daunting for anyone. Croizon managed it without arms or legs. He did not wear prostheses on his arms, but he did have special flippers attached to his legs.

BETTER THAN THE REAL THING?

Some people believe that today's most advanced prostheses are so effective they could provide the wearers an unfair advantage over able-bodied athletes. Unlike muscles and other natural body parts, prostheses do not tire out. They can also be specially designed for maximum effectiveness at a certain sport. Markus

Rehm, whose right leg is amputated below the knee, faced this issue in 2014. Officials excluded the German long jumper from his country's national track-and-field team. They argued that Rehm's prosthesis might give him an advantage over other competitors.

Other athletes have encountered similar resistance. The controversy over whether to allow amputees to compete with able-bodied people is likely to continue for some time. It is a complicated issue. However, this debate's existence is evidence that prostheses have progressed to a truly amazing level. ✳

Swimmer Philippe Croizon practices moving underwater with prosthetic flippers in place of legs.

During a sports physical, doctors might test a patient's heart rate and breathing during exercise.

AVOIDING INJURIES

Even with all the latest breakthroughs in sports medicine, it is better, of course, to prevent injury in the first place. Sports medicine professionals help athletes practice correct form and strengthen their bodies. This helps the athletes endure the rigors of competition.

Before starting a new sport, many athletes schedule a sports physical. This examination helps determine whether a person is physically prepared to play a certain sport. A doctor examines a patient's medical history and tests his or her physical fitness. The doctor might recommend certain training or exercise before the patient dives into full competition. The doctor might also inform the patient of potential risks associated with the sport and offer advice on how to avoid injury. Sports physicals are especially common for younger athletes. This is because their bodies are still growing and changing, putting them at risk for a variety of lasting injuries.

EVERYDAY HEALTH TECHNOLOGY

New technology is making it easier for athletes to monitor their own bodies and stay healthy. For example, a number of wearable electronic devices can automatically track wearers' heart rates, how far they travel during exercise sessions, how much energy their bodies burn, and more. Some devices can even monitor how well a person sleeps, an important sign of physical health. Such devices often take the form of a lightweight bracelet.

Athletes in contact sports such as hockey or football have started upgrading their headgear. Special sensors monitor head impacts. If a blow is potentially dangerous, the sensors blink a warning.

There are even thermometers in pill form, designed for a person to swallow. They track a person's body temperature. This helps an athlete know when they've become overheated. They may need to rest and cool down or drink more fluids.

SMART PHONE TRACKS AND DISPLAYS HEALTH INFO

WEARABLE DEVICE MEASURES HEART RATE, DISTANCE, AND OTHER USEFUL INFORMATION

Smartphone apps and other computer software help athletes monitor their exercise programs and physical health.

Treating an injury often requires help from many different health care professionals.

3

IT TAKES A TEAM

The field of sports medicine is a broad area of study. Within this field are many areas of specialization. Some sports medicine doctors focus solely on head injuries while others treat muscles and bones. Sports psychologists focus on the **psychology** of athletes, helping them keep a positive attitude as they recover. Therapists assist patients during their recoveries and may help them learn to move again. Nurses provide a range of additional care to patients.

In many situations, it takes an entire team to treat an injury and put an athlete back in the game. A patient might see a number of doctors, therapists, and other medical professionals over the course of the treatment. Each one of these highly trained experts plays an integral role in helping the patient make a full recovery.

SUCCESS STORIES

1976	1985	2012	2013
Tommy John returns to Major League Baseball after the first ever UCL reconstruction surgery.	Basketball legend Michael Jordan makes a stunning return after sitting out 65 games in a row due to a broken foot.	Runner Oscar Pistorius becomes the first double amputee to compete in the Olympic Games.	Football star Peyton Manning has the best season of his career after sitting out the entire 2011 season due to a neck injury.

DIFFERENT DOCTORS

Sometimes athletes suffer from pain or another condition that does not require emergency care. Their first stop is probably with a general practitioner, also known as a primary care physician. This is the same kind of doctor you might see if you aren't feeling well and need some medicine or other basic care. A general practitioner might be able to treat some sports-related ailments, depending on the specific issues involved.

In cases that require specialized treatment, a general practitioner may refer patients to an orthopedist or a physiatrist. An orthopedist is a doctor who specializes in treating muscles and bones. A physiatrist is a doctor who works with patients during their **rehabilitation** after an injury. Depending on the nature of an injury, other specialists might be involved in a patient's treatment as well. Sometimes these doctors work at specialized sports medicine clinics. Other times they treat a variety of patients, both athletes and otherwise.

An orthopedist or physiatrist might show x-rays or other medical images to patients to help explain an injury.

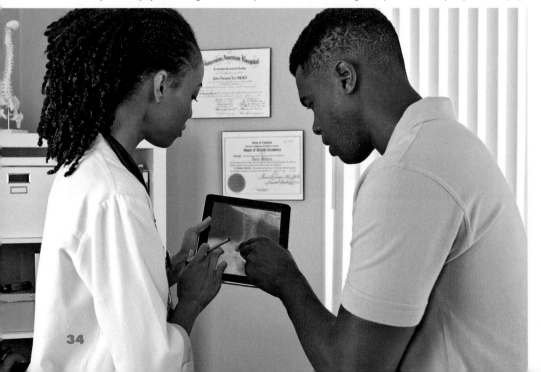

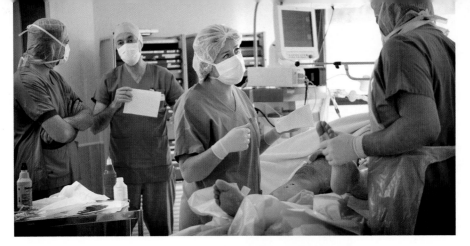

A team of surgeons, nurses, and assistants works together to complete operations.

SURGICAL SPECIALTIES

There are also doctors who specialize in surgical procedures. Surgeons focus on a certain part of the body. For example, there are orthopedic surgeons who specialize in knees and others who specialize in shoulders. Even within these specializations, most surgeons dedicate themselves to a handful of specific procedures. Surgeons might perform the same operation thousands of times over the course of their careers.

The job of a surgeon is demanding and stressful. Even more than other doctors, surgeons must be very good at working with their hands. All surgical procedures require very precise movements. Even the smallest mistake could result in serious injury to the patient. In some cases, it could be life-threatening. Surgeons must also be able to concentrate intently for long periods of time. Some procedures can take several hours to complete. Being able to stay calm in these stressful situations is an important part of being a surgeon.

JAMES ANDREWS

Dr. James Andrews (1942–) is one of the best-known sports surgeons in the world. He has performed more than 40,000 operations over the course of his career to repair injured knees, shoulders, and elbows. His patients have included superstars from just about every major sport, from NFL and National Basketball Association players to pro wrestlers.

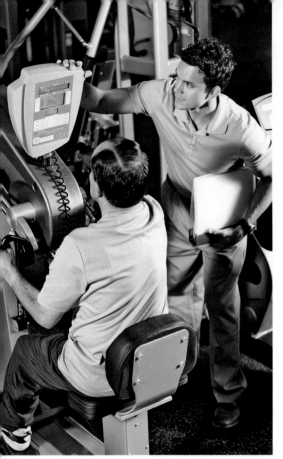

Physical therapy is a crucial part of the recovery process for most sports injuries.

PHYSICAL THERAPY

Physical therapists play a crucial role in helping athletes stay healthy. They are experts in how different types of movement affect the body. Therapists collect a lot of information to diagnose injuries and develop treatment plans. They examine their patients' medical history, watch them move, and talk to them about the pain and other feelings they experience as they move. They also feel the patient's body with their hands. Sometimes all it takes to help an athlete is to teach that person the correct way to move while playing sports or exercising. Other times, a therapist might recommend a conditioning program to increase muscle strength or flexibility.

Therapists also help patients increase strength and flexibility during the rehabilitation process. Thus, a physical therapy session for a patient recovering from surgery might involve anything from walking on a treadmill to lifting weights or stretching. Over the course of rehabilitation, a therapist observes the patient's progress and adjusts the exercises as needed. The therapist can also perform hands-on techniques to adjust the alignment of a patient's muscles and bones and relieve pain.

NURSING

Nurses are extremely important in every medical specialty, and sports medicine is no exception. Doctors make the final decisions about a patient's diagnosis or how a patient should be treated. But nurses often spend more time directly interacting with patients. They gather information, perform tests, and administer basic treatments to patients. Nurses perform a range of tasks, from recording a patient's vital signs to giving injections and drawing blood for tests.

Like doctors, some nurses specialize in certain areas. For example, there are nurses who dedicate themselves to helping surgeons operate on patients. They prepare patients for surgery, make sure the surgeon has all the necessary tools, and more.

Nurses might help with tasks such as showing a patient how to put on a brace.

THE ARTISTIC SIDE

Running shoes are designed to grip surfaces while offering cushion and support to the runner's feet and ankles.

THE RIGHT GEAR FOR THE GAME

A big part of staying healthy while exercising or playing sports involves using the right kind of equipment. For example, there are special kinds of shoes for just about every athletic activity. Pads and helmets protect vulnerable body parts in contact sports. Braces provide additional support to joints.

STAYING COMFORTABLE

Modern sportswear also keeps athletes comfortable. Some special materials help absorb excess sweat and keep an athlete's skin dry. Others are designed to allow as much air as possible to flow through, keeping the athlete cool.

Stretchy, breathable materials keep athletes comfortable and cool.

A good bicycle helmet can protect against head injuries while allowing plenty of air to pass through, keeping the rider's head cool.

Some activities are easiest when athletes don't have a lot of excess fabric on their bodies. For example, gymnasts, dancers, and swimmers often wear skintight, stretchy materials. These provide the maximum amount of flexibility possible. Tights can also help athletes stay warm in cold weather without needing to wear bulky, heavy clothing.

LOOKING GOOD

Of course, even while they are sweating and exerting themselves, people like to look good. In addition to being functional, they want their sportswear to be stylish. A trip to a sneaker shop or sporting goods store will reveal a nearly endless selection of designs in many different colors, sizes, and shapes. There is something for everyone.

Just as with clothes created for other situations, sports apparel is envisioned by creative designers. They study fashion trends and brainstorm new and exciting looks for athletic gear. In fact, some athletic gear is so fashionable that people wear it even when they aren't exercising. Many high-fashion designers have even incorporated ideas from sportswear into their own creations for the fashion runway. ☀

ATHLETIC TRAINING

For athletes, staying healthy is not always about going to the doctor. It also involves proper training and conditioning to make sure their bodies are prepared. Sports teams, schools, and gyms employ athletic trainers to provide guidance for how to stay physically fit. An athletic trainer might work with a sports team to develop personalized exercise plans for each member. These trainers also teach how to avoid injuries. For example, many athletes from basketball players to gymnasts must learn how to land properly to prevent ACL injuries.

Athletic trainers can provide basic medical care when needed. They are also able to diagnose many common sports injuries, including concussions. They are often the people who assess whether it is safe for an athlete to return to play. However, they are not doctors. When an athlete under a trainer's care is seriously injured, part of the trainer's job is to make sure the athlete sees a doctor for the proper treatment.

A trainer keeps an eye on an athlete's form and training routine to help her avoid injury.

Nutritionists know that eating the right foods in the right amounts is an important part of keeping athletes healthy.

ADDRESSING DIETARY NEEDS

Maintaining a healthy diet is another big part of staying in shape and avoiding injury. All athletes must be careful to eat foods that fuel their activities and to drink plenty of fluids to stay hydrated. Many athletes with specific goals consult with food experts called dieticians and nutritionists. These professionals have a detailed understanding of the way different foods can affect the body. They know what people should eat, when they should eat it, and how much they should eat.

Some athletes want to lose weight to become lighter and more agile. Others want to pack on the pounds as they build enormous muscles. Dieticians and nutritionists can help them plan out meals or decide which foods should be avoided. These experts analyze how much energy different athletes use and how much food they need to stay healthy and competitive. Clients' tastes also play a role in designing the right diet. If clients don't like the foods they're eating, they are more likely to give up their diets and eat what they want.

AN INTERVIEW WITH PHYSICAL THERAPIST DARIN SWAN

Darin Swan is a physical therapist at PeaceHealth Southwest Medical Center in Vancouver, Washington. He specializes in helping patients recover from sports injuries.

When did you start thinking you wanted to be a physical therapist? Did any person or event inspire that career choice?
I started thinking I wanted to be a physical therapist in high school. I played many sports growing up and was always interested in the rehabilitation of injured athletes and sports medicine as a whole. When I injured my shoulder in high school basketball, I went through the injury recovery process and was impressed with all the knowledge and skills that were utilized by the physical therapist.

What kinds of classes should a would-be therapist look to take in middle school, high school, and beyond? Being a good physical therapist requires a good understanding of general medicine as a foundation. Courses in biology, chemistry, physics, and **anatomy** and physiology [the study of how the body functions] can be taken in middle school and high school. In college and in preparation for physical therapy school, you will want to consider more advanced classes in anatomy and physiology, exercise physiology, biology, kinesiology, and psychology.

What other projects and jobs did you do in school and your work life before you became a physical therapist? How did that work prepare you for your career?
In middle school, I did a presentation on the mechanics of the golf swing. It explained how to improve power, efficiency, and accuracy with a reduced risk of injury. This movement analysis process has become my greatest passion in my job today. I have expanded my knowledge base and skill set to work with runners, bicyclists, baseball pitchers, and golfers. I have been able to make a huge impact in people's quality of life by teaching them to do these activities with speed, strength, and efficiency while reducing the risk of injury.

In high school and college, I worked as a physical therapist aide in outpatient physical therapy clinics, in order to learn as much as I could about rehabilitating musculoskeletal injuries. These jobs helped me realize how much I enjoyed helping people return to full function in athletics, physically demanding jobs, and activities of daily living.

It takes teamwork to treat patients effectively. Does working as part of a team come naturally to you, or was it something you had to work on? Working as a part of a team did not come naturally at first. Early in my career, I wanted to work independently and demonstrate my competency and skills to my clients and move up the ladder of success on my own two feet. Over time, I learned that practicing in a vacuum without colleagues nearby to help you learn and grow was a big mistake. My current clinic has developed a culture of learning where this process of commiserating [sympathizing] with fellow physical therapists on difficult cases helps us provide the highest quality of care and ensures the best outcomes for our patients.

Have you ever worked with an athlete who made an especially amazing recovery? I worked with a young man who served in the military and lost his leg below the knee. His goal was to return to running. After he was fitted for a blade runner prosthesis [a type of prosthesis specially designed for running], we were able to do a running gait video analysis, which helped him to understand how he could run again with the aid of this prosthesis and without knee and hip pain.

What is the most satisfying part of working as a physical therapist? The most satisfying part of my job is when I can decrease a person's pain and help them return to the activities that they love, live for, and are passionate about. When you improve someone's quality of life and they express their appreciation of your knowledge, skills, and compassion, it is a very rewarding experience.

What advice would you give a young person who wants to be a physical therapist one day? Find a job or volunteer as a physical therapy aide in a clinic or hospital setting. Shadow a physical therapist as they work with patients, and ask them what they like most about their job and what they find challenging. This type of experience in the field will help you determine if physical therapy is a good fit for you.

A variety of science classes are required in the education of any medical professional.

IN THE CLASSROOM

Like all medical professionals, people involved in sports medicine need a strong knowledge of science. In high school, they might take classes in biology, chemistry, and physics. In college, they continue to study these subjects, with a special focus on human anatomy.

After earning a bachelor's degree, athletic trainers need special certification from the National Athletic Trainer Association to start working. Many also go on to earn a master's degree. Physical therapists complete a three-year graduate program to earn a Doctor of Physical Therapy degree. Students who want to become doctors must attend medical school for at least four years. Some specialties require several years of additional training after this. Nurses can begin working after earning an associate's degree, though many go on to earn bachelor's, master's, and doctorate degrees.

All medical professionals must be licensed in the state where they practice. Becoming licensed requires earning the appropriate degrees and passing exams. Some states require medical professionals to complete additional education throughout their careers. This enables them to keep up-to-date with the latest medical advancements.

ADDITIONAL TRAINING

Becoming successful as a doctor, therapist, or any other practitioner in the medical field requires a lot more than just studying from a book or listening to teachers in a classroom. Hands-on experience is a major part of education in the medical world. There is no way to truly learn how to treat a patient without actually doing it. Most medical students begin gaining this experience by volunteering at hospitals or doctors' offices during high school or college. This gives them a close look at what it is like to work in health care.

While studying to become a doctor, therapist, or nurse, hands-on experience is built into the curriculum. For example, medical students spend several years of their education working under the supervision of experienced doctors. Therapists and nurses also spend time working in clinical settings under supervision during their education. People working in medical careers are only allowed to graduate and become licensed after proving that they are able to provide care effectively.

Sports doctors and therapists also have to understand the special needs of someone who is dedicated to athletic activity. As a result, many are athletes themselves. Playing a variety of sports and staying in good physical shape can be very helpful for people who want to work in the sports medicine field.

On-the-job training gives health care professionals the experience they need to treat patients effectively.

Socccer players are prone to knee injuries.

4

GETTING BACK IN THE GAME

"Over here!" Amy shouted as she ran toward the goal, signaling to her teammate Beth that she was open and ready for a pass. Beth kicked the ball to Amy, who expertly caught it along the inside of her foot. Amy began to dribble forward. Within an instant, she had positioned herself for a perfect shot at the goal. She planted her left foot firmly at the side of the ball and swung her right leg back in preparation for the kick. However, as she began to bring her leg forward, Amy realized that something wasn't quite right. She heard a popping sound and felt her left knee begin to give out. Just as her right foot made contact with the ball, she fell to the ground. Amy clutched at her injured knee, which was in pain and beginning to swell. She could already tell that she wouldn't be able to walk off the field without help.

THE ROAD TO ACL RECOVERY

week 1	week 2	week 6	week 12	weeks 26-39
Surgery takes place; patient begins physical therapy.	Patient no longer needs crutches.	Patient begins more intense exercises using weights.	Patient can begin jogging and sport-specific training.	Healing is complete.

DISCOVERING THE PROBLEM

As the ball drifted out of bounds, the referee blew her whistle to stop the game. The athletic trainer for Amy's team ran out onto the field to see if she was okay. Right away, the trainer could tell that Amy would need to see a doctor. She had seen similar injuries before, and she knew this wasn't something that would go away on its own.

At the doctor's office, Amy went through a number of simple tests. She lay on her back as the doctor moved her leg into different positions, felt around the knee joint, and asked Amy questions about her pain. In just a few minutes, the doctor was fairly certain that Amy had torn her ACL. To be sure the diagnosis was correct, he scheduled her for an MRI later that week. He also gave her a pair of crutches and recommended that she avoid putting any weight on her leg.

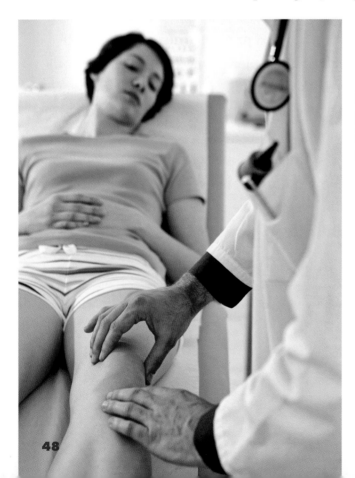

Sometimes a doctor might only need to feel a patient's knee with his or her hands to accurately diagnose an injury.

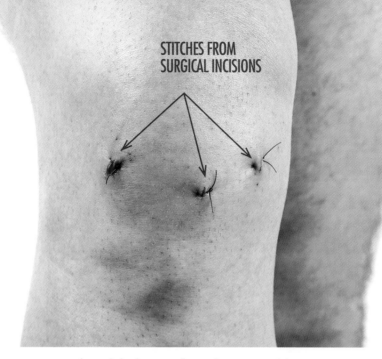

STITCHES FROM
SURGICAL INCISIONS

ACL reconstruction surgery leaves behind very small wounds on a patient's knee.

TREATMENT TIME

After Amy's MRI, her doctor received a report showing the results. They confirmed his diagnosis of a torn ACL. He explained to Amy that she would need to undergo ACL reconstruction surgery. The surgery would involve removing the damaged ACL and replacing it with a tendon from the body of an organ donor. Over time, the tendon would form a strong bond with Amy's leg bones and take the place of her ACL.

At first, Amy was scared. What if she wasn't able to run or play soccer anymore? However, her doctor assured her that it was a common procedure. With time and the right therapy, Amy was likely to make a full recovery.

Amy's doctor referred her to an orthopedic surgeon who was well known in the area for performing this procedure. Though she was still a little scared of having an operation on her knee, Amy knew she would be in good hands.

LASTING CONTRIBUTIONS

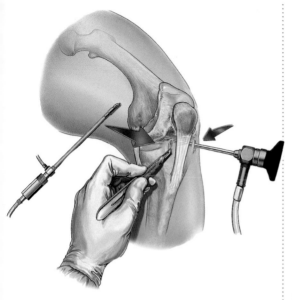

Arthroscopic surgery gives a surgeon full access to the knee without large incisions.

ARTHROSCOPIC SURGERY

ACL reconstruction and many other types of joint surgery are usually performed using arthroscopic surgery. In this style of surgery, a doctor begins by making a small incision, or cut. Then a tiny, tube-shaped video camera is inserted into the patient's body. The doctor can then look at a screen to see the interior of the patient's joint. With the camera in place, the surgeon can make additional incisions. Tiny surgical tools are inserted. The surgeon performs the surgery by watching the video screen while manipulating the tools.

WHAT ARE THE BENEFITS?

Arthroscopic surgery offers major benefits to athletes. Because it only requires very small incisions, less damage is done to the patient's body during surgery. This can significantly decrease the time it takes the patient to recover. It is also less painful and less likely to leave extensive scars behind. Finally, it does not require a long hospital stay. Many patients are even able to go home the same day they receive the operation.

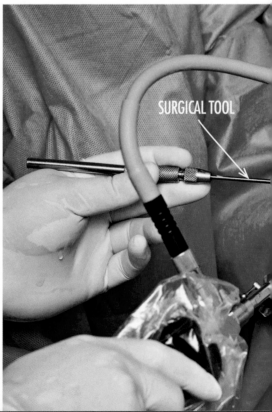

SURGICAL TOOL

THE ORIGINS OF ARTHROSCOPY

The roots of arthroscopic surgery lie in Dr. Maximilian Nitze's 1879 invention of a device called a cystoscope. The cystoscope was a small, tube-shaped device that could be inserted into the body. A doctor looked through one end and could see inside.

In 1918, Dr. Kenji Takagi surgically inserted such a device into the knee joint of a **cadaver**. This was the beginning of

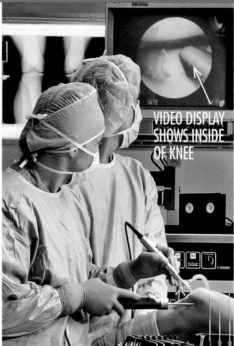

VIDEO DISPLAY SHOWS INSIDE OF KNEE

During surgery, the surgeon keeps an eye on the video screen as he or she moves the tools to complete the operation.

arthroscopy. (The term *arthroscopy* comes from the Greek words for "joint" and "look.") Over time, other doctors began to improve on Takagi's idea. They built arthroscopes that were better suited to examining joints. Finally, in the 1970s, the invention of small television cameras led to the creation of arthroscopes very similar to the ones used now.

Arthroscopy is considered one of the most important surgical advances of the past century. It is an important tool for orthopedic surgeons not just in treating athletes, but in treating any patients who need surgery on their joints. ✴

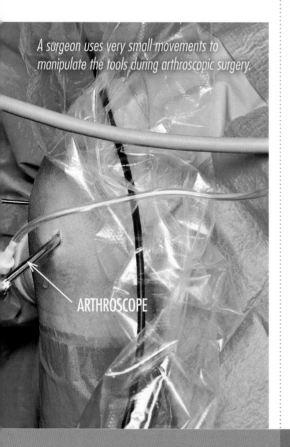

A surgeon uses very small movements to manipulate the tools during arthroscopic surgery.

ARTHROSCOPE

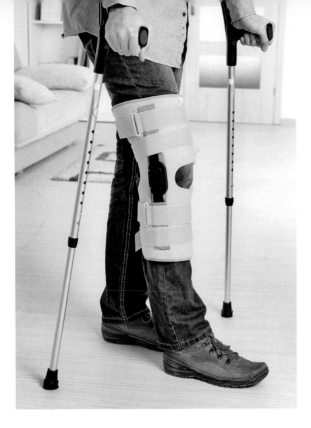

A knee brace keeps a patient from bending a healing joint too far.

THE HEALING PROCESS

Just as the doctor had promised, Amy's surgeon was a true expert at ACL reconstruction. She was able to complete the procedure quickly and smoothly, with no complications. After the surgery, she told Amy that it looked like everything was going to be fine eventually. However, Amy would have a long road of healing ahead of her. As Amy's surgeon left, a nurse came in to teach her how to avoid infection and take care of the bandages around her knee.

Before Amy left the hospital, she met with a physical therapist. He gave her a brace to wear around her knee and showed her how to put it on. He explained that it would provide support as the joint began to heal. He also showed her how it would limit the range of motion on her leg to keep her from bending it too far and ruining the surgery. Finally, he recommended some basic exercises she could start doing right away to help begin the healing process.

SMALL STEPS

Around a week after the surgery, Amy's knee was still painful. However, she was already starting to feel like she could put more weight on it. She met again with her doctor and her physical therapist, who both told her that the pain was normal. They were happy with the way her knee was healing, and they agreed that she was ready to start the next phase of healing. From then on, Amy regularly met with the therapist, who specialized in helping athletes. The therapist helped her use exercises to strengthen the muscles around her knee. Within two weeks, she no longer needed crutches to help her stand. She could also bend and stretch her knee more. Therapy was a lot of work. Amy had to do squats, ride an exercise bike, and lift weights. Each time she saw the therapist, the workouts got harder. She was tired out after every appointment. However, she knew that the only way to get back on the soccer field was to work hard and do everything the therapist asked of her.

At first, a recovering patient might avoid putting too much weight on the injured joint.

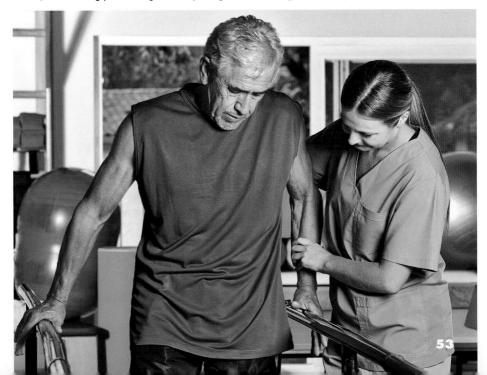

WHERE THE MAGIC HAPPENS

A huge staff of talented researchers works on many different projects at Langone's facilities.

NYU LANGONE SPORTS MEDICINE CENTER

Some of today's top sports medicine experts can be found hard at work at the Sports Medicine Center of New York University's (NYU) Langone Medical Center. A division of Langone's Center for Musculoskeletal Care, the Sports Medicine Center is one of the country's most advanced sports medicine facilities. Thousands of surgeries are performed there each year. They range from common procedures such as an ACL reconstruction to more cutting-edge treatments. The center's doctors treat professional and top-level athletes from around the nation.

RESEARCH AND TRIALS

Doctors at Langone do more than treat patients. They also conduct research on everything from new surgical techniques to discovering new information about how the body works. Its Musculoskeletal Research Center is equipped with specialized

Researchers might connect patients to special equipment to measure their body's reactions to different kinds of exercise.

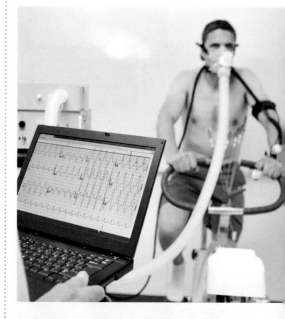

The experts at Langone have treated a full range of athletes, including professional dancers.

laboratories with the latest scientific technology. This enables doctors to perform a huge variety of tests and experiments. In addition, patients can sign up to participate in clinical trials for experimental treatments. This allows doctors to try out new treatment methods to ensure that they will work properly.

It's at places like this, as well as at other universities and hospitals around the world, where innovative new medications and treatments are developed. One day, doctors here could make the next big breakthrough in sports medicine!

THE NEXT GENERATION

Langone is part of NYU's School of Medicine and plays an important role in training new doctors. As one of the country's top medical schools, NYU attracts some of the best students from all around the world. These students learn from the experienced doctors at the center. They also help with research projects. This helps the students build the knowledge they need to one day become experts in their own right. ✹

A therapist might show a patient how to do stretches that assist in the healing process.

EASING BACK IN

Throughout her physical therapy program, Amy met regularly with her doctor to check on her progress. Each time, he moved her leg around and asked her if she was feeling any pain. This helped him make sure that the new tendon in Amy's leg was attaching to her bones successfully. He also looked at notes from the physical therapist to see how Amy was doing with her exercises. This information helped the doctor decide when she could start participating in more intense activities.

Over time, Amy's therapy sessions became less frequent. The therapist began to work with her on more soccer-related exercises. He taught her about using proper form and technique while playing so she could avoid reinjuring herself in the future. He also gave her a list of exercises to do on her own. Amy continued to work hard. Before long, she started to feel like her old self again.

STAYING SAFE

About nine months after her surgery, Amy was back in her soccer uniform and taking warm-up shots. In just a few minutes, she and her team would take the field for the first game of the new season. Amy was nervous. She had been training and practicing with her teammates for weeks now. But this would be her first time playing in a real game since the injury.

As it turned out, Amy didn't have anything to worry about. As she played, she remembered everything her therapist taught her about proper form. She was even able to score a goal late in the game, giving her team a 2–1 victory. As her teammates high-fived and celebrated, Amy breathed a sigh of relief. Her months of training had paid off, and she knew she would be able to play just as well as she had before tearing her ACL. Thanks to the skills and knowledge of her doctors, physical therapist, and other sports medicine professionals, she was back in the game.

With the right treatment, an injured athlete can return to the field and play just as well as before the injury.

THE FUTURE

Preventive care can help athletes avoid many injuries altogether.

Like all areas of health care, the field of sports medicine is constantly evolving. Doctors, scientists, and engineers are always hard at work. Their work produces new technology, equipment, and techniques to keep athletes—and even nonathletes—healthy and strong. It is hard to predict exactly what breakthroughs will come next. However, there are a few trends that show where sports medicine might head in the coming years.

PREVENTIVE CARE

Sports doctors have long stressed the importance of preventive care. This involves regular examinations and tests, even when an athlete shows no obvious symptoms of injury. Sports doctors know that problems discovered in their earliest stages are more easily treated. In the past, most insurance plans have not provided coverage for this sort of care. However, this is beginning to change. More people are realizing the

Better helmets could help protect football players from devastating brain injuries.

long-term benefits of preventing injuries from becoming serious in the first place. In the future, sports doctors and therapists will likely devote more time to preventing injuries than to rehabilitation.

BETTER EQUIPMENT

In recent years, there has been a great deal of controversy over the number of serious brain injuries suffered by professional football players. Many of these athletes get concussions regularly. While the players usually recover quickly, recent studies have shown that head injuries can have lasting effects. This is true even for "minor" concussions, particularly if a person does not fully recover from one concussion before experiencing another. Many retired NFL players suffer from memory loss and other mental problems.

As a result, there has been a new effort to protect football players and other athletes who engage in contact sports. Engineers are working on new types of helmets. Their goal is to design helmets that are lightweight and comfortable yet strong enough to protect players from concussions. ✺

CAREER STATS

PHYSICIANS AND SURGEONS

MEDIAN ANNUAL SALARY (2012): $187,200

NUMBER OF JOBS (2012): 691,400

PROJECTED JOB GROWTH: 18%, faster than average

PROJECTED INCREASE IN JOBS (2012–2022): 123,300

REQUIRED EDUCATION: Doctoral or professional degree

LICENSE/CERTIFICATION: Must be licensed; requirements vary between states

PHYSICAL THERAPISTS

MEDIAN ANNUAL SALARY (2012): $79,890

NUMBER OF JOBS (2012): 204,200

PROJECTED JOB GROWTH: 36%, much faster than average

PROJECTED INCREASE IN JOBS (2012–2022): 73,500

REQUIRED EDUCATION: Doctoral or professional degree

LICENSE/CERTIFICATION: Must be licensed; requirements vary between states

ATHLETIC TRAINERS AND EXERCISE PHYSIOLOGISTS

MEDIAN ANNUAL SALARY (2012): $42,690

NUMBER OF JOBS (2012): 28,900

PROJECTED JOB GROWTH: 19%, faster than average

PROJECTED INCREASE IN JOBS (2012–2022): 5,400

REQUIRED EDUCATION: Bachelor's degree

LICENSE/CERTIFICATION: Must be licensed or certified in most states; requirements vary between states

Figures reported by the United States Bureau of Labor Statistics

RESOURCES

BOOKS

Bell, Samantha. *Sports Medicine Doctor*. Ann Arbor, MI: Cherry Lake Publishing, 2016.

Harasymiw, Therese. *A Career as a Physical Therapist*. New York: Rosen Publishing, 2015.

FACTS FOR NOW

Visit this Scholastic Web site for more information on sports medicine:
www.factsfornow.scholastic.com
Enter the keywords **Sports Medicine**

GLOSSARY

anatomy (uh-NAT-uh-mee) the scientific study of the structure of living things

archaeologists (ahr-kee-AH-luh-jists) people who study the distant past, which often involves digging up old buildings, objects, and bones and examining them carefully

cadaver (kuh-DA-vur) a dead body

concussion (kuhn-KUHSH-uhn) an injury to the brain caused by a heavy blow to the head

diagnose (dye-uhg-NOHS) to determine what disease or other medical issue a patient has or what the cause of a problem is

gait (GAYT) a way of walking

inflammation (in-fluh-MAY-shuhn) redness, swelling, heat, and pain, usually caused by an infection or injury

ligament (LIG-uh-muhnt) a tough band of tissue that connects bones and holds some organs in place

neurological (noor-uh-LAH-jih-kuhl) of or having to do with the brain

orthopedic (or-thuh-PEE-dik) of or having to do with the branch of medicine that deals with bones and joints

paralysis (puh-RAL-i-sis) a loss of the power to move or feel a part of the body

physicians (fi-ZISH-uhnz) people with a medical degree who have been trained and licensed to treat injured and sick people

prosthesis (prahs-THEE-sis) an artificial device that replaces a missing part of a body

psychology (sye-KAH-luh-jee) the study of the mind, the emotions, and human behavior

radiation (ray-dee-AY-shuhn) atomic particles that are sent out from a radioactive substance

rehabilitation (ree-huh-bi-luh-TAY-shuhn) the restoration of something to a former state

sterilization (ster-uh-li-ZAY-shuhn) the ridding of something of germs and dirt by exposing it to heat or chemicals

tendon (TEN-duhn) a strong, thick cord or band of tissue that joins a muscle to a bone or other body part

INDEX

Page numbers in *italics* indicate illustrations.

American Board of Medical Specialties, 7

American College of Sports Medicine, 7

amputees, 28–29, *28, 29,* 33, 43

ancient athletes, 8, *8,* 12, *12*

ancient doctors, 10–11, *10, 11, 12,* 13

Andrews, James, 35

anterior cruciate ligament (ACL), 16, 47, 48, 49, *49,* 50, 52, 54, 57

antigravity treadmills, 19, 25, *25*

arthroscopic surgery, 50–51, *50–51*

athletic trainers, 40, *40,* 48

brain injuries, 17, *17,* 26, 59, *59*

bursitis, 20

clothing, 38–39, *38*

Croizon, Philippe, 28, *29*

cystoscopes, 51

dieticians, 41

education, 42, 43, 44, *44,* 45, *45,* 55

exoskeletons, 19, 26, *26*

force plates, 27

gait analysis, 27, *27,* 43

Galen, Claudius, 13

general practitioners, 34

helmets, *18,* 38, *39,* 59, *59*

Hippocrates, 11, *11*

inflammation, 20

iontophoresis, 20, *20*

Jobe, Frank, *14,* 15

John, Tommy, *14,* 15, *15,* 33

Jordan, Michael, 33

knee braces, *6,* 52, *52*

knee injuries, *24,* 27, 35, *46,* 47, 48, *48,* 49, *49*

Langone Medical Center, 54, *54,* 55, *55*

licensing, 44, 45

magnetic resonance imaging (MRI), *22–23,* 23, 48, 49

Manning, Peyton, 33

monitoring devices, 31, *31*

Musculoskeletal Research Center, 54–55

Nadal, Rafael, 21

neurological damage, 26

Nitze, Maximilian, 51

nurses, 33, *35,* 37, *37,* 44, 45, 52

nutritionists, 41, *41,*

Olympic Games, 12, 13, *13,* 33

orthopedists, 34, *34*

Paralympic Games, 28

phonophoresis, 20

physiatrists, 34, *34*

physical examinations, 30, *30*

physical therapists, 36, *36,* 42–43, 44, 45, 52, 53, *53,* 56, *56*

Pistorius, Oscar, 33

platelet-rich plasma, 19, 21, *21*

Polamalu, Troy, 21

posture, 27

preventive care, 58–59, *58*

prostheses, 28–29, *28, 29,* 43

radiologists, *23*

rehabilitation, 25, *25,* 34, 36, *36,* 42, 43, 47, 50, 52, 53, *53,* 56, *56,* 58

Rehm, Markus, 29

research, 10, 54–55, *54*

Röntgen, Wilhelm Conrad, 22

Rose, Derrick, *6*

INDEX *(CONTINUED)*

shoes, 38, *38*
shoulder injuries, 20, 35, 42
specialization, 8, 12, 13, *23,*
    33, 34, 35, 37
sports physicals, 30, *30*
surgeons, 10, 15, 35, *35,* 37,
    50, 52
surgery, 15, 16, 24, *24,* 25,
    33, 35, *35,* 37, 47, 49, *49,*
    50–51, *50–51,* 52, 54
Swan, Darin, *42,* 42–43

Takagi, Kenji, 51
Tarentum, Iccus of, 7

tendinosis, 17
transducers, 23
treadmills, 19, 25, *25,* 36

ulnar collateral ligament (UCL),
    14, 15, 33
ultrasound, 23

Woods, Tiger, 21

x-rays, 19, 22–23, *22, 34*

ABOUT THE AUTHOR

JOSH GREGORY is the author of more than 90 books for kids. He has written about everything from animals to technology to history. A graduate of the University of Missouri–Columbia, he currently lives in Portland, Oregon.